MW01168527

1

Author photo credit: Cherrybird Photography

Psalms for a Season of Grief

Psalm 71:20-21

You who have shown me many troubles

and distresses will revive me again,

and will bring me up again from the depths of the earth.

In memory of

Jonah L. Baker,

our guardian angel

August 29, 2016 to February 20, 2018

Contents

Foreword

About three years after the death of our beloved son Jonah, I finally feel the courage and strength to put together some thoughts about our grieving process to try and encourage others. I used to feel that I was completely alone in my grief, but I've met several other couples who have also been through the loss of a child. It is a loss that is indescribable and seems to violate the very laws of natural order in the world. Only another parent who has experienced the same terrible loss would know what it truly feels like.

Our son was eighteen months old when he passed away from a rare condition called hemophagocytic lymphohistiocytosis (HLH), which has a very poor prognosis and a survival rate of only 55%. He was treated with chemotherapy, but didn't have a good response to it. For a long time, we really wondered "has God forgotten to be merciful? Has he withheld his compassion?" as it was written in Psalm 77.

In recent years, watching some of my friends go through the loss of a parent unexpectedly, or go through a divorce and mourn the loss of that relationship and the life that had been planned together, I learned that grief and loss can take several forms.

All of us have been through or will probably go through grief at some point in our lives, which makes it universal. And yet there is still a solitude about grief that makes it feel like the loneliest road possible. We often don't know how to seek help for ourselves, or to help others who are grieving. We don't know what to say or do.

Finding resources for grief was especially difficult after our loss. A few of my friends shared books with me that were helpful, and perhaps one of the most insightful works on grief was "A Grief Observed," by C.S. Lewis, which he wrote after the loss of his dear wife. I was encouraged to share my own perspectives on grief, from some reflections on the book of Psalms. The book of Psalms conveys lament, despair, fear, and anguish, just as much as it expresses praise or thanksgiving. It is truly a

fitting book for anyone calling out to God with anger, confusion, anxiety, and grief.

One of the most helpful things that someone said to me after my son died was to "have patience with your grief." Unlike other advice at the time, this seemed to acknowledge that what happened to me was tremendous, and that there was nothing anyone could say or do to make it better right away. Allow your grief to be what it is, allow yourself to feel it for as long as you need to, and don't rush to get over it.

Although I have a special place in my heart for parents going through the loss of a child, and those who are experiencing miscarriage or infertility, I do write this book for anyone who is going through any grief or loss, no matter what form it takes, and no matter what triggered it.

Psalm 77:1-12

I cried out to God for help;

I cried out to God to hear me.

When I was in distress, I sought the Lord;

at night I stretched out untiring hands,

and I would not be comforted.

I remembered you, God, and I groaned;

I meditated, and my spirit grew faint.

You kept my eyes from closing;

I was too troubled to speak.

I thought about the former days,

the years of long ago;

I remembered my songs in the night.

My heart meditated and my spirit asked:

"Will the Lord reject forever?

Will he never show his favor again?

Has his unfailing love vanished forever?

had his promise failed for all time?

Has God forgotten to be merciful?

Has he in anger withheld his compassion?"

Then I thought, "To this I will appeal:

the years when the Most High stretched

out his right hand.

I will remember the deeds of the Lord;

yes, I will remember you miracles of long ago.

I will consider all your works

and meditate on all your mighty deeds."

Parallel Universes

The world of the pediatric intensive care unit was like a parallel universe that I never planned or wanted to be a part of. For the 50 days that my son was in the intensive care unit, it was an ongoing nightmare that I could not escape from. I still remember the tubes and lines that were connected to him, the sounds of the ventilator and dialysis machines, the doctors and nurses coming in and out of his room at all times of the day and night. I remember sleeping in a corner behind his hospital crib and taping a calendar on the wall where we would mark down medical events that happened during the day—dialysis, PICC line clogged, antibiotics started, intubation, lumbar puncture, brain MRI, bone marrow biopsy, the first day of chemotherapy, positive blood cultures, palliative care consult.

I also remember the other families that were there, the ones who had been there much longer than we had been, the ones who lost their children to devastating illnesses as well. I would never have known about those families or children, or even been aware that such a stressful place existed if our own child hadn't needed to be there.

After our son passed away, we were introduced to an older couple who had also lost a child when they were around our age. We were grateful to meet another couple who had been through a similar ordeal and didn't feel as alone anymore as a result of talking to them. They were able to understand our pain and grief in a way that others couldn't. They were also able to give us encouragement and advice after decades of processing their own grief.

None of us would ever ask for grief to enter our lives. As much as we hate broadening our perspectives through personal pain and loss, we are able to relate more to others who are going through similar suffering. Grief does open our eyes to another aspect of the human experience. In the early stages of grief, we can't imagine anything good coming out of our grief at all. God feels very far away, out of reach, and

we wonder "why, Lord, do you stand far off? Why do you hide yourself in times of trouble?" (Psalm 10).

One day we may be at the point where we are one of the comforters that are able to help others through their suffering much more deeply because of the empathy and understanding that we have. For now, just focus on your own feelings and emotions. Seek out others who have been through similar grief in support groups or acquaintances.

"Since her grief had brought her fully to birth and wakefulness in this world, an unstinting compassion had moved in her, like a live stream flowing deep underground, by which she knew herself and others and the world." [Wendell Berry]

Psalm 10:1, 14

Why, Lord, do you stand far off?

Why do you hide yourself in times of trouble?

You, God, see the trouble of the afflicted;

you consider their grief and take it in hand.

Psalm 57:1-3

Have mercy on me, my God,

have mercy on me,

for in you I take refuge.

I will take refuge in the shadow of your wings

until the disaster has passed.

I cry out to God Most High,

to God, who vindicates me.

He sends from heaven and saves me,

rebuking those who hotly pursue me—

God sends forth his love and his faithfulness.

Reflection questions:

1. If you were in a hospital with your loved one towards the end of his or her life, what were the most difficult things about that experience?

2. What did you see during your loved one's illness that opened your eyes to things you were never aware of in the world?

The Greatest Mystery

What happens after death is still the greatest mystery, where we go and how it might feel in those final moments of consciousness. Seeing our loved one depart is a traumatic experience. After months of illness, it may even have been somehow a relief when the suffering finally ended. The face and body may not look like what we expect death to be like. It's not like how it looks on television or in the movies.

Dying may not have looked peaceful or natural. I remember hearing choking and gurgling sounds, and seeing colors on my baby's face that were blue, yellow, and purple. I still have nightmares about his last moments, when he struggled to breathe, then finally let go. I felt his spirit depart. In that moment, I realized that the body is just a vessel for carrying the spirit. After death, the body becomes a completely meaningless shell, even after we have nursed it and fussed over it all along.

Our loved one may be buried in a cemetery or cremated with his or her remains in an urn, but we wonder where they are physically. Jonah's urn sits on a shelf in our room, but it's strange to think of him being trapped inside that golden jar. I think of him as being with God the creator, made completely whole and happy.

I meditate on the verse from Psalm 84: "Blessed are those who dwell in your house; they are ever praising you," because as much as I want him back here with me on earth, I know he is in a much better place. I also sometimes picture him as a humongous blue whale, floating freely in the ocean, strong and healthy once again.

Psalm 27:4

One thing I ask from the Lord, this only do I seek:

that I may dwell in the house of the Lord

all the days of my life, to gaze on the beauty of the Lord

and to seek him in his temple.

Psalm 84

How lovely is your dwelling place, Lord Almighty!

My soul yearns, even faints, for the courts of the Lord;

my heart and my flesh cry out for the living God.

Even the sparrow has found a home,

and the swallow a nest for herself,

where she may have her young—a place near your altar,

Lord Almighty, my King and my God.

Blessed are those who dwell in your house;

they are ever praising you.

Blessed are those whose strength is in you,

whose heart are set on pilgrimage.

As they pass through the Valley of Baka,

they make it a place of springs;

the autumn rains also cover it with pools.

They go from strength to strength,

till each appears before God in Zion.

Hear my prayer, Lord God Almighty; listen to me, God of Jacob.

Look on our shield, O God;

look with favor on your anointed one.

Better is one day in your courts than a thousand elsewhere;

I would rather be a doorkeeper in the house of my God

than dwell in the tents of the wicked.

For the Lord God is a sun and shield;

the Lord bestows favor and honor;

no good things does he withhold

from those whose walk is blameless.

Lord Almighty, blessed are those who trust in you.

Reflection questions:

1. What scared or traumatized you about the way your loved one died?

2. What thoughts or feelings do you have about where his or her spirit may be now after death?

Funeral Plans

If you've ever planned a funeral for your baby, you know you are part of a special minority group of parents, and not special in a good way. At the time of crisis when wounds are fresh and time is most needed for mourning, there are unfortunate logistics that need to be discussed. One of them is how to honor the life of the person you loved through a funeral or memorial service, and it may feel like you can't ever do enough to commemorate the beautiful life that was lived. In our case, we tried to capture the joy of our son even though his life was short, only 18 months long. We wanted to help him build a legacy and share the things he loved with others, but we weren't sure how.

We truly felt that we were "walking through the darkest valley," as described in Psalm 23. It can be so overwhelming trying to handle people during this sensitive time, and we felt pressured to respond to everyone who reached out to us to let them know we appreciated them.

Give yourself permission to keep the funeral small, only family and close friends if needed, and to give yourself space away from others. I often felt like I had to be strong enough to be there for others, like my family and friends who flew in from other states for the funeral, but looking back, it would have been better to just focus on my own emotions and feelings. Get the help of your church pastor in planning the funeral or giving a eulogy if you don't feel strong enough to be the one to deliver it.

Psalm 23

The Lord is my shepherd, I lack nothing.

He makes me lie down in green pastures,

he leads me beside quiet waters,

he refreshes my soul.

He guides my along the right paths for his name's sake.

Even though I walk through the darkest valley,

I will fear no evil,

for you are with me;

your rod and your staff,

they comfort me.

You prepare a table before me

in the presence of my enemies.

You anoint my head with oil;

my cup overflows.

Surely your goodness and love will follow me

all the days of my life,

and I will dwell in the house of the Lord forever.

Reflection questions:

1. In what ways do you need help from your community of family and friends to overcome logistics like planning the funeral, and receive comfort after your loss?

2. In what ways do you also need solitude and space away from other people during this sensitive period of time?

Routines

When we got back home after the funeral, two of Jonah's bath towels were still hanging up in his room on the closet door, waiting for him to come home and take a bath that night. I pressed my face into them to take a deep whiff of the lavender scent that reminded me of him. We loved using that purple shampoo and lotion on him. His hair was always so soft and smelled like honey and lavender.

For months, the towels still hung in the same place and collected dust. After a few months, I finally and hesitantly took them down and washed them. What did this signify? I don't know. Maybe nothing. Or maybe part of me had finally accepted that he would not be coming back again, ever.

The thing about death is that it is final, and can't be undone. I hold onto memories, photographs, strands of his hair from his first haircut, handprints made from clay, his artwork, because they are all I have left—precious relics. His purple shampoo, which I uncap and sniff sometimes, brings me back to happier times.

Our grief counselor told us that the "acceptance" stage of grief is not just accepting that your loved one has died. That's the "easy" part. She said that the hard part is accepting how your life is going to be from now on without that person. It feels like I may never fully reach that stage.

For months, my husband and I walked around as if in a daze, unsure what to do with our time. We were so used to our schedules revolving around our child—waking him up in the morning, changing his diapers, feeding him, getting him to sleep for naptimes, and cleaning up after he played. Without that structure, we were suddenly back to being two married people without a child again, which felt so strange and empty. I understood what the psalmist wrote in Psalm 13, lamenting "how long must I wrestle with my thoughts, and day after day have sorrow in my heart?"

One of the things that helped me with my grieving was to establish a routine where I took care of myself again, physically and emotionally. I would exercise, meet with my friends, and try to get enough sleep. My husband and I worked on routines like going on date nights together and reconnecting with one another.

"The person one loves should take all their things with them when they die."
[Gabriel Garcia Márquez, Love in the Time of Cholera]

Psalm 13:1-5

How long, Lord?

Will you forget me forever?

How long will you hide your face from me?

How long must I wrestle with my thoughts

and day after day have sorrow in my heart?

How long will my enemy triumph over me?

Look on me and answer, Lord my God.

Give light to my eyes, or I will sleep in death,

and my enemy will say, "I have overcome him,"

and my foes will rejoice when I fall.

But I trust in your unfailing love;

my heart rejoices in your salvation.

Psalm 56:8

Record my misery;

list my tears on your scroll;

are they not in your record?

Reflection questions:

1. What part of your daily routine do you miss the most after the loss of your loved one?

2. How can you focus your routine on self-care during this difficult time?

Unanswered Prayers

Does it feel like God answered everyone's prayers except yours? Were you worried that if you "didn't pray hard enough" or "didn't have enough faith," that God wouldn't hear you? We were really hoping for a "medical miracle" when Jonah was sick, and for a short time it did seem like he was improving in the hospital. Then things took a turn for the worse when he had complications from chemotherapy, and we were told the inevitable truth that he would die no matter what treatments he received.

I felt so much anger and abandonment from God at that point. Our friends and pastors from church would come to gather and pray for us. It all seemed to fail. Psalm 35 says "when my prayers returned to me unanswered, I went about mourning" and "I bowed my head in grief."

After about two years of struggling with this question of unanswered prayers, I heard a sermon from a pastor who talked about God answering our prayers in ways we don't expect. Yes, I had wanted God to save Jonah's physical body from illness so that he could stay with us on earth and we could watch him grow up. What I realized is that God did something much bigger. He had saved Jonah's soul eternally, through the sacrifice of his son Jesus, so that we could be together always in heaven one day. I saw the larger picture of God's story, and how our story does not end when we die here on earth.

When I think about examples of unanswered prayers from the Bible, I remembered that Jesus had prayed to God before he died. Before he was crucified, Jesus prayed, "My father, if it is possible, let this cup pass from me; yet not as I will, but as You will" (Matthew 26:39). God didn't answer his son Jesus' prayer, not because he didn't pray hard enough, had little faith, or wasn't favored by God, but because he had a bigger plan for humanity that would take place through Jesus.

There is a temporary goodbye when we lose a loved one, but there is hope of reuniting someday when we all return to God. We will never understand why our prayers weren't answered the way we wanted them to

be during our time here on earth, and that will always be a mystery on this side of heaven, but we will eventually see the bigger story when we are finally with God on the other side.

Psalm 35:13-14

When my prayers returned to me unanswered,

I went about mourning as though for my friend or brother.

I bowed my head in grief as though weeping for my mother.

Psalm 42:1-5, 9-11

As the deer pants for streams of water,

so my soul pants for you, my God.

My soul thirsts for God, for the living God.

When can I go and meet with God?

My tears have been my food day and night,

while people say to me all day long, "Where is your God?"

These things I remember as I pour out my soul:

how I used to go to the house of God

32

under the protection of the Might One

with shouts of joy and praise among the festive throng.

Why, my soul, are you downcast?

Why so disturbed within me?

Put your hope in God, for I will yet praise him,

my Savior and my God.

I say to God my Rock, "Why have you forgotten me?

Why must I go about mourning,

oppressed by the enemy?"

My bones suffer mortal agony as my foes taunt me,

saying to me all day long,

"Where is your God?"

Why, my soul, are you downcast?

Why so disturbed within me?

Put your hope in God, for I will yet praise him,

my Savior and my God.

Reflection questions:

1. In what ways do you feel like you have been forgotten or forsaken by God?

2. What does scripture say about God's love and promises for us? Write the scripture here.

Loss of Identity

More than just losing a loved one, grief means you have lost a major part of your identity, and a part of your life that really defined you. What did you lose as a result of the death of a loved one? Were you a daughter or a son, and feel like your identity as a child has changed? Were you someone's spouse and feel like your other half was taken away? Were you someone's best friend and miss the conversations and fun that you used to have with that person?

When my son passed away, I felt like my identity as a mother had been torn apart. One of my friends told me that "once you walk through the door of motherhood, you never walk back." I felt like I was still a mother, but without a child to love. I felt like my entire purpose and significance had been taken away, and I felt lost every day. It didn't feel worth it to go to work, clean the house, or do anything because every task felt utterly meaningless.

Psalm 31 says "I am forgotten as though I were dead; I have become like broken pottery." I felt exactly like a piece of broken pottery that was previously part of something whole and intact, and was now shattered on the ground.

The death of my son made me question all my other identities as well. Mother, wife, daughter, doctor, student, friend. Who was I, really, when these roles could be so easily stripped away? After meditation and prayer, I realized the one identity that could never be taken away is that I am a child of God. Even when other relationships can be broken or ended, and underneath all the layers that define us in our daily lives, we were still fundamentally created by God and loved by God.

As terrible as grief is, it has the purifying power of removing all the worldly things that we use to identify ourselves with. Grief is a time when we can go to God with the simplest and most humble version of ourselves—as his beloved child.

Psalm 31:1-10, 12

In you, Lord, I have taken refuge;

let me never be put to shame;

deliver me in your righteousness.

Turn your ear to me,

come quickly to my rescue;

be my rock of refuge,

a strong fortress to save me.

Since you are my rock and my fortress,

for the sake of your name lead and guide me.

Keep me free from the trap that is set for me,

for you are my refuge.

Into your hands I commit my spirit;

redeem me, Lord, my faithful God.

I hate those who cling to worthless idols;

as for me, I trust in the Lord.

I will be glad and rejoice in your love,

for you saw my affliction and knew the anguish of my soul.

You have not given me into the hands of the enemy

but have set my feet in a spacious place.

Be merciful to me Lord,

for I am in distress;

my eyes grow weak with sorrow,

my soul and body with grief.

My life is consumed by anguish and my years by groaning;

my strength fails because of my affliction,

and my bones grow weak.

I am forgotten as though I were dead;

I have become like broken pottery.

Reflection questions:

1. What aspect(s) of your identity feel the most broken as a result of your loss?

2. How can you find comfort in your identity as God's child during this difficult time?

God Knows Our Beginning and Our End

One of the things that we can frequently feel guilty about after we lose a loved one is whether or not we could have done anything differently to change the outcome. I often felt weighed down by guilt when I wonder whether I could have caught my son's condition at an earlier stage or if he could have survived had his treatment been different during his hospital stay.

The possibility of "what if" became so strong that I started going back farther and farther in time, even questioning my marriage and whether my husband and I were doomed from the beginning somehow. It almost became an obsession to pinpoint the exact moment in time when things started going downhill, eventually leading to the death of our child.

One of the questions our counselor earnestly asked us was "do you feel like you could have done things better to prevent your son from getting sick?" And the answer was "yes," because I feel like as a mother I should have known that he was seriously ill and needed help sooner. And the answer was also "no," because I did everything I knew how to do at the time, and we were sent home a couple times from the emergency room because nothing serious was suspected. We were told all kids get sick and they all bounce back. I know that I could not control or foresee everything because I am not God; I can only do what I am able to do as a limited human being.

Our grief counselor shared with us that she felt a lot of guilt about the circumstances surrounding her mother's death, because she felt like a lot of things towards the end of her mother's life could have been handled better. She shared that after years of guilt and self-punishment, she heard the Holy Spirit saying that "God knows our beginning and our end." This means that we still do our due diligence and act as responsibly as possible, but sometimes God still calls a loved one home at a certain time and we can't stop that.

I struggle with this delicate concept because I am a doctor, and after so much training about safety and avoiding mistakes in medical practice, it feels like there is always something more we can do to prevent loss of human life and unnecessary suffering.

At the same time, I have also seen the limitations of medicine and how death can still happen despite all preparation and intervention. In the end, I choose to believe that God does know how we are born and how we will die. Even if we had done things differently, God would probably still have called our son home to heaven at that time. Know that you did everything you could at the time with the information and tools that you had. If you could have done more for your loved one, you certainly would have.

Psalm 139 says that "all the days ordained for me were written in your book before one of them came to be." I still go through "what if" scenarios in my mind, but with an inability to change the past, I trust in God's ultimate plan even if I don't fully understand it.

Psalm 139:1-16

You have searched me, Lord,

and you know me.

You know when I sit and when I rise;

you perceive my thoughts from afar.

You discern my going out and my lying down;

you are familiar with all my ways.

Before a word is on my tongue

you, Lord, know it completely.

You hem me in behind and before,

and you lay your hand upon me.

Such knowledge is too wonderful for me, too lofty for me to attain.

Where can I go from your Spirit?

Where can I flee from your presence?

If I go up to the heavens, you are there;

if I make my bed in the depths, you are there.

If I rise on the wings of the dawn,

if I settle on the far side of the sea,

even there your hand will guide me,

your right hand will hold me fast.

If I say, "Surely the darkness will hide me

and the light become night around me,"

even the darkness will not be dark to you;

the night will shine like the day,

for darkness is as light to you.

For you created my inmost being;

you knit me together in my mother's womb.

I praise you because I am fearfully and wonderfully made;

your works are wonderful, I know that full well.

My frame was not hidden from you

when I was made in the secret place.

When I was woven together in the depths of the earth,

your eyes saw my unformed body.

All the days ordained for me were written in your book

before one of them came to be.

Reflection questions:

1. What regrets are you carrying around and torturing yourself with?

2. With time and prayer, how can you slowly let go of those regrets and trust that things happened how God willed them to be?

Jesus Wept

One of our greatest fears during grieving is that nobody cares about our suffering, and that even God doesn't care. We are afraid to face what happened to our loved one was just a random cruel act of nature and natural selection or that we are just a random speck in the galaxy or universe and our suffering means nothing and goes unnoticed even by God.

This is not true. There are many instances in the Bible when God tries to show us that he personally cares about our tragedies and not only grieves with us, but grieves even more than we do because it was one of his precious children that passed away.

A church pastor pointed us to a passage about Lazarus. John 11:33-35 says: *"When Jesus saw her weeping, and the Jews who had come along with her also weeping, he was deeply moved in spirit and troubled. 'Where have you laid him?' he asked. 'Come and see, Lord,' they replied. Jesus wept. Then the Jews said, See how he loved him!"*

Jesus knew that He was about to revive Lazarus, but He still wept because He had empathy for His friend and for the suffering of the family members. God also weeps over the death of your loved one, and is with you as you weep. Illness and death were not part of God's dream for his creation.

The Lord does "hear our cries for mercy" and "turns his ear to us" (Psalm 116). He catches your tears in a bottle and knows the number of hairs on your head. There is not a sparrow that falls without God seeing it happen. God does know the depth of your sorrow and grief more than anyone, and mourns alongside you.

Psalm 116

I love the Lord, for he heard my voice, he heard my cry for mercy.

Because he turned his ear to me, I will call on him as long as I live.

The cords of death entangled me,

the anguish of the grave came over me;

I was overcome by distress and sorrow.

Then I called on the name of the Lord: "Lord, save me!"

The Lord is gracious and righteous;

our God is full of compassion.

The Lord protects the unwary;

when I was brought low, he saved me.

Return to your rest, my soul, for the Lord has been good to you.

For you, Lord, have delivered me from death,

my eyes from tears, my feet from stumbling,

that I may walk before the Lord in the land of the living.

I trusted in the Lord when I said, "I am greatly afflicted,"

in my alarm I said, "Everyone is a liar."

What shall I return to the Lord for all his goodness to me?

I will lift up the cup of salvation and call on the name of the Lord.

I will fulfill my vows to the Lord

in the presence of all his people.

Precious in the sight of the Lord

is the death of his faithful servants.

Truly I am your servant, Lord,

I serve you just as my mother did,

you have freed me from my chains.

I will sacrifice a thank offering to you

and call on the name of the Lord.

I will fulfill my vows to the Lord

in the presence of all his people,

in the courts of the house of the Lord—

in your midst, Jerusalem.

Praise the Lord.

Reflection questions:

1. What are ways you feel unseen or abandoned by God in your grief?

2. How can you ask God through prayer and by reading scripture to show his love and empathy to you?

Physical Grief

Besides the emotional and mental trauma of losing a loved one, the body can suffer in a multitude of ways during grief and mourning. I remember feeling a sense of severe and chronic fatigue during the year that followed my son's death. It was as if my body were physically weighed down by sandbags and the force of gravity felt much stronger than before. I experienced insomnia even though I was drained and tired, had low appetite, and lost weight.

I congratulated myself for small things I was able to do during that period of time. If I even got out of bed in the morning to go to work, I was proud of myself. I didn't take much time off work after the funeral, even though a lot of people do, and maybe I should have. Slowly over time I started an exercise routine again, walking outside, sleeping better, and feeling better bit by bit.

I have seen a lot of patients develop a condition called fibromyalgia, which is widespread and chronic debilitating pain after an extremely traumatic event. The connection between mind, body, and spirit is deeply intricate and events that impact us emotionally can manifest through physical symptoms. You may experience body aches, fatigue, low or increased appetite, lack of sleep or too much sleep, frequent headaches, stomach and digestive issues, weight gain or weight loss, among other symptoms.

Make sure you take care of your own health during this time. Meeting with a grief counselor can help you process heavy emotions and thoughts that weigh you down. Meditate on Psalm 73, which says that "my flesh and my heart may fail, but God is strength of my heart and my portion forever."

Psalm 6:2-7

Have mercy on me, Lord, for I am faint;

heal me Lord, for my bones are in agony.

My soul is in deep anguish.

How long, Lord, how long?

Turn, Lord, and deliver me;

save me because of your unfailing love.

Among the dead no one proclaims your name.

Who praises you from the grave?

All night long I flood my bed with weeping

and drench my couch with tears.

My eyes grow weak with sorrow;

they fail because of all my foes.

Psalm 73:23-26

Yet I am always with you;

you hold me by my right hand.

You guide me with your counsel,

and afterward you will take me into glory.

Whom have I in heaven but you?

And earth has nothing I desire besides you.

My flesh and my heart may fail,

but God is the strength of my heart and my portion forever.

Reflection questions:

1. What physical symptoms or health issues have you been experiencing during the grieving process?

2. How can you better take care of your body and mind during this difficult time?

Holidays

Holidays and special occasions are some of the worst days after you lose someone you love. Everyone else is out celebrating and being merry while you are hiding away and mourning.

I remember that the first holiday we encountered after my son passed away was Easter. Not only was it terrible seeing all the Easter decorations for kids displayed in the grocery stores, we didn't feel at all ready to celebrate Easter Sunday and to notice the arrival of spring. We were entering a dark winter season in our lives that felt out of sync with everyone else's joy and hope.

After Easter came Mother's Day, which was also horrible. Then came my birthday, which I didn't even want to celebrate that year because I felt like dying. Later in the year came Halloween, which is geared towards children, and another sad day for us. Even worse were Christmas and New Year's Eve. Having a Christmas tree without presents underneath the tree for our son felt so wrong. I remember that was the worst holiday season of our lives because reminiscing on the past year felt so painful. We weren't excited to usher in a new year at all.

Remembering the central message of those holidays and special occasions helped me. With Easter, it's not actually about the Easter bunny and the candy baskets that children receive. Easter is actually about how Jesus conquered death and is victorious over illness and our mortality on earth. Mother's Day is not just about receiving some flowers and a card. It's about how a woman's life is changed forever when she nurtures new life into this world, and how the bond between a mother and child can never be erased, no matter what happens.

Holidays and special occasions continue to be difficult days for us. We prepare ourselves emotionally ahead of time and give each other plenty of grace. I try to remember the meaning of those days in the context of God's forever kingdom. "When my spirit grows faint within me, it is you who watch over my way" (Psalm 142). I also imagine that my son is celebrating those days with us while he is in heaven.

52

Psalm 22:1-2, 9-11

My God, my God, why have you forsaken me?

Why are you so far from saving me,

so far from the words of my groaning?

My God, I cry out by day, but you do not answer,

by night, but I find no rest.

Yet you brought me out of the womb;

you made me feel secure on my mother's breast.

From birth I was cast on you;

from my mother's womb you have been my God.

Do not be far from me, for trouble is near

and there is no one to help.

Psalm 142:1-3

I cry aloud to the Lord, I lift up my voice to the Lord for mercy.

I pour out before him my compliant;

before him I tell my trouble.

When my spirit grows faint within me,

it is you who watch over my way.

Reflection questions:

1. If there are holidays or special occasions coming up, how can you give yourself permission to celebrate as little or as much as you feel comfortable with?

2. Are there any special rituals or traditions you and your family would like to incorporate into special occasions to honor the memory of your loved one so you don't feel like you are leaving them out?

The World Keeps Spinning

One of the cruelest things about the world is that it continues to move on, despite the magnitude of your tragedy. Your entire world just crumbled, your whole personal life is destroyed and burned to the ground. Yet the traffic still goes on past your window, people still go to work, everyone seems normal at the grocery store, and nobody stopped or even blinked an eye in consolation.

Meanwhile you're screaming on the inside that your child just died in a horrific way and your life is shattered. It seems like the world should slow to a halt, if only for a day, and mourn together in silence, but it never happens. Other people go on having a normal day, and may even seem celebratory or happy while you feel completely disoriented. Nothing is normal for you and it feels like life will never be normal again. You wish you could push pause on life to rest and hide for a while, but the bills still need to be paid and dinner still needs to be made.

Give yourself a break and take some time off from work and seeing people if you need to. Go for a walk at the park, meditate, spend time alone with your spouse. You may want to "hurry to a place of shelter, far from the tempest and storm" (Psalm 55). Go on a trip for a little while if you need to get away from the house and all the belongings that your loved one left behind at home.

Psalm 55:1-8, 22

Listen to my prayer, O God,

do not ignore my plea;

hear me and answer me.

My thoughts trouble me and I am distraught

because of what my enemy is saying,

because of the threats of the wicked;

for they bring down suffering on me

and assail me in their anger.

My heart is in anguish within me;

the terrors of death have fallen on me.

Fear and trembling have beset me;

horror has overwhelmed me.

I said, "Oh, that I had the wings of a dove!

I would fly away and be at rest.

I would flee far away

and stay in the desert;

I would hurry to my place of shelter,

far from the tempest and storm."

Cast your cares on the Lord

and he will sustain you;

he will never let the righteous be shaken.

Reflection questions:

1. How does it feel like the world is forever changed for you, yet remains normal for everyone else?

2. What are ways you can devote time to yourself and take a break from the regular pace of life?

Dark Nights

Grief is difficult during the daytime, but at least we can try to stay busy and talk to people around us if we want to. Nights are especially difficult and agonizing during the acute process of grief. It is at night that we feel our solitude and desperation the very most. I remember having a lot of insomnia after my son passed away, tossing and turning with feelings of anger, sorrow, regret, or guilt. I didn't have anyone to talk to because my husband was a deep sleeper and I felt bad calling any of my friends in the middle of the night.

I also had a lot of nightmares and flashbacks about my son's hospital stay and funeral during those days. My subconscious had developed a lot of cobwebs and dark corners. I was most vulnerable to spiritual attacks at night and had really dark thoughts about whether life was really worth living without my son. At night I felt that "tens of thousands assailed me on every side" (Psalm 3). It was during this period of time that I started doing more journaling, meditation, and yoga at night before bed to relax my body and mind.

I discovered sleep meditation recordings on YouTube. There is an especially helpful man named Jason Stephenson who makes tons of free sleep meditations videos on YouTube for overcoming insomnia. There is also a Christian meditation app called "Abide" that uses scripture-based tools to help you unwind your mind and anxiety at night or at any time. I would highly recommend using these to help ease any tension or anxiety you are experiencing at night.

Psalm 3:3-6

But you, Lord, are a shield around me,

My glory, the one who lifts my head high.

I call out to the Lord,

and he answers me from his holy mountain.

I lie down and sleep;

I wake again, because the Lord sustains me.

I will not fear though tens of thousands assail me on every side.

Psalm 4:1, 8

Answer me when I call to you,

my righteous God.

Give me relief from my distress;

Have mercy on me and hear my prayer.

In peace I will lie down and sleep,

for you alone, Lord,

make me dwell in safety.

Reflection questions:

1. How does the solitude and darkness of nighttime affect your grief?

2. What are ways you can lessen the severity of your sorrow at night and ease your anxiety before falling asleep?

60

Stewardship, Not Ownership

One thought I often wrote in my journal was that "it isn't fair that God stole Jonah from our lives." I felt like an innocent child did not need to die to prove whatever point or lesson that God had to show us about the world or our lives. It didn't make sense that God would give him to us, then take him away just as quickly. The death of our child felt like some inviolable rule of the universe had been broken.

I eventually realized that God is not able to steal anything, because everything and everyone on earth belongs to him. Psalm 24 says that "the earth is the Lord's, and everything in it, the world, and all who live in it." We are asked to be good stewards of the people and things that God entrusts to us during our time here on earth. The truth is that every life ultimately belongs to God.

For some reason, God called Jonah home back to heaven much sooner than he called other people back home. What was the reason for that? I don't have a clue. Somehow, we try to trust that God is still good and has a good plan for everything.

In the end, we will all return to God, and our time here on earth is borrowed time. Sometimes the anxiety I have over the possibility of losing another loved one can become crippling. Sometimes I can even idolize my loved ones, like my husband or daughter, and feel like I can't live life without them. I can place their importance above God because they mean so much to me. This is when I try to remember that my loved ones ultimately belong to God, and he has the best intentions and plans for them. I try to remember that my life is borrowed too, and I am meant to live to glorify God in both good and bad times.

Psalm 24

The earth is the Lord's, and everything in it,

the world, and all who live in it;

for he founded it on the seas and established it on the waters.

Who may ascend the mountain of the Lord?

Who may stand in his holy place?

The one who has clean hands and a pure heart,

who does not trust in an idol or swear by a false god.

They will receive blessing from the Lord

and vindication from God their Savior.

Such is the generation of those who seek him,

who seek your face, God of Jacob.

Lift up your heads, you gates; be lifted up, you ancient doors,

that the King of glory may come in.

Who is this King of glory?

The Lord strong and mighty, the Lord mighty in battle.

Lift up your heads, you gates; lift them up, you ancient doors,

that the King of glory may come in.

Who is he, this King of glory?

The Lord Almighty—he is the King of glory.

Reflection questions:

1. In what ways do you feel like you had ownership of your loved one?

2. How can you shift your perspective to one of stewardship of the time you had with your loved one until he or she returned to the Creator?

Bit By Bit

There is a quote by the musician Eric Clapton that helped me immensely. He lost his son when he tragically fell out of the window of a New York apartment building at the age of three. I felt an immediate kinship with him and all other parents who have experienced a devastating event like that. Eric Clapton's quote is that *"I have a huge pool of grief, and once in a while, I dip a toe in it."*

After I read that, I gave myself permission to feel small amounts of grief at a time and deal with it a bit at a time instead of letting it hit me all at once constantly. Sometimes that is not possible, and the weight of it all crashes down on you and you can't wish it away even if it's extremely overwhelming. But know that you are allowed to process one piece of your grief at a time, to take breaks and think about other things as well.

You don't have to face the entirety of your situation all at once, and your loved one would want you to find pearls of joy and peace from time to time even though they are gone. Slowly, God will "lift you out of the slimy pit, out of the mud and mire" and "give you a firm place to stand" (Psalm 40).

Psalm 40:1-3, 11

I waited patiently for the Lord;

he turned to me and heard my cry.

He lifted me out of the slimy pit,

out of the mud and mire;

he set my feet on a rock

and gave me a firm place to stand.

He put a new song in my mouth,

a hymn of praise to our God.

Many will see and fear the Lord

and put their trust in him.

Do not withhold your mercy from me, Lord;

may your love and faithfulness always protect me.

Reflection questions:

1. What are some activities or blocks of time you can set aside to do something you enjoy once in a while?

2. How can you approach difficult days a little at a time?

Oceans and Tides

Shortly after our son passed away, my husband and I took a road trip out west, just the two of us. We visited several cities on the way from the Midwest to the West Coast. We made it out to see the ocean in San Diego, Monterey, Portland, Seattle, and other towns along our drive on famous highway 101. We would write our son's name in the sand as a remembrance ritual wherever we went.

The ocean teaches me different things each time I see it. In the past, it showed me how vast and infinite God is, and how deep and wide his love is for us. This time when I looked at the ocean, what it showed me was the continual ebb and flow of our lives. The waves rush in, and rush out. The tide comes in and goes out. Just like our lives and experiences, the waves never stay constant—they are always moving and changing.

It is the same with grief. There are times we feel okay, like life is bearable, and then there are times of feeling completely crushed and devastated. You could be feeling fine one minute, then a wave of grief will wash over you out of the blue, with or without a trigger. We want our grief to progress linearly towards a resolution, but it helps to think of grief as having more of a cyclical nature, an ebb and flow.

One day could be considered a setback, but the next day could be much better. Eventually, the size and force of the waves do lessen over time. The waves don't feel like tsunamis anymore, and one day they may even feel like small ripples.

Life never stays constant; it always keeps flowing, always moves us through triumphs and tragedies and back again, and it never stays still. "You who have shown me great troubles and distresses will revive me again, and will bring me up again from the depths of the earth" (Psalm 71).

Psalm 18:1-6, 16, 19

I love you, Lord, my strength.

The rock is my rock, my fortress and my deliverer;

my God is my rock, in whom I take refuge,

my shield and the horn of my salvation, my stronghold.

I called to the Lord, who is worthy of praise,

and I have been saved from my enemies.

The cords of death entangled me;

the torrents of destruction overwhelmed me.

The cords of the grave coiled around me;

the snares of death confronted me.

In my distress I called to the Lord;

I cried to my God for help.

From his temple he heard my voice;

my cry before him, into his ears.

He reached down from on high and took hold of me;

he drew me out of deep waters.

He brought me out into a spacious place;

he rescued me because he delighted in me.

Psalm 71:20-21

You who have shown me many troubles

and distresses will revive me again,

and will bring me up again from the depths of the earth.

May you increase my greatness and turn to comfort me.

Reflection questions:

1. How do you feel your grief changing through the course of a day, week, or month?

2. What are triggers for waves of grief and how can you prepare for them?

The Loneliest Road

Grief can cause social isolation and solitude. Maybe you don't want to see people as much anymore because you feel depressed and can't interact with other people normally. It can also feel like you are being left out of social events. For a while we were afraid of being left out of our friends' kids' birthday parties and events like baby showers. I am sure friends were trying to be considerate to us during a sensitive time. It also felt like grief was putting a wedge between us and everyone else who hadn't experienced something so tragic. Whether real or imaginary, I felt the truth of what was written in Psalm 38 when it says that "my friends and companions avoid me because of my wounds; my neighbors stay far away."

I was nervous about seeing people again, especially people within our church community. It felt like people wanted to say something helpful but just didn't want to say the wrong thing, so they avoided us. I didn't want to drag others down when they seemed so happy and normal, whereas my entire world and perspectives had changed. The only people we talked to on a regular basis during the initial period of grieving were other couples who knew what it was like to be in our shoes. They became our new best friends.

Through our pastors, we were introduced to other couples who had been through a similar experience. We were appreciative of being introduced and brought together with the kindest and most gracious group of people, when we otherwise would never have met.

Psalm 38:11

My friends and companions avoid me because of my wounds;

my neighbors stay far away.

Psalm 25:16-22

Turn to me and be gracious to me, for I am lonely and afflicted.

Relieve the troubles of my heart and free me from my anguish.

Look on my affliction and my distress

and take away all my sins.

See how numerous are my enemies

and how fiercely they hate me!

Guard my life and rescue me;

do not let me be put to shame,

for I take refuge in you.

May integrity and uprightness protect me,

because my hope, Lord, is in you.

Redeem Israel, O God,

from all their troubles!

Reflection questions:

1. In what ways do you feel like grief has separated you from other people?

2. How can your community link you to others who have been through similar experiences and can talk to you to give you hope?

Blame

In our deep grief and search for a palpable reason for the misfortune of what happened to us, we can start blaming other people. We are so desperate to make some sense of what happened that we grasp for any answers. I sympathize with all the women throughout history who were blamed for experiencing infertility, miscarriage, or other tragedies. Not only did they feel the full weight of their grief, but they were also blamed for their misfortune, or they blamed themselves.

Spouses often start to blame each other for events leading up to the illness and/or death of their child. This is why the divorce rate for couples who have experienced the loss of a child is reported to be so high. The couples seem to either come together and lean on each other during their grief, or they use each other as scapegoats for the disaster. I am guilty of having a spirit of blame toward my husband for a while after our son died.

I was also the recipient of blame. My mom blamed us because she didn't want our son to receive chemotherapy from the pediatric oncologists. She wanted to use natural methods and traditional Chinese medicine which we didn't agree with at the time. She also blamed us after our daughter was born and said that we didn't dress her properly or feed her right, and she was sure to get sick, just like Jonah did.

It caused us to be estranged for a period of time because she made our grief much, much worse. The way she was acting didn't make sense to me for a long time and I wished I had more support from her during an already difficult time. She also removed all traces of Jonah from her house, like his photos and artwork, and never mentioned his name ever again.

Eventually I realized that she doesn't have healthy ways of processing her grief and took it out on us instead, which was not right, but that happens when people don't receive the help they need through counseling and other methods. Over a long period of time, I had to learn to forgive

myself for my shortcomings and forgive others during their time of grief as well. Psalm 130 reminds me that "with [God] there is forgiveness, so that we can, with reverence, serve [him]."

Psalm 86

Hear me, Lord, and answer me,

for I am poor and needy.

Guard my life, for I am faithful to you;

save your servant who trusts in you.

You are my God; have mercy on me, Lord,

for I call to you all day long.

Bring joy to your servant, Lord,

for I put my trust in you.

You, Lord, are forgiving and good,

abounding in love to all who call to you.

Hear my prayer, Lord;

listen to my cry for mercy.

When I am in distress, I call to you,

because you answer me.

Among the gods there is none like you, Lord;

no deeds can compare with yours.

All the nations you have made

will come and worship before you, Lord;

they will bring glory to your name.

For you are great and do marvelous deeds;

you alone are God.

Teach me your way, Lord,

that I may rely on your faithfulness;

give me an undivided heart,

that I may fear your name.

I will praise you, Lord my God, with all my heart;

I will glorify your name forever.

For great is your love toward me;

you have delivered me from the depths,

from the realm of the dead.

Psalm 130:1-4

Out of the depths I cry to you, lord;

lord hear my voice.

Let your ears be attentive to my cry for mercy.

If you, lord, kept a record of sins, lord, who could stand?

But with you there is forgiveness,

so that we can, with reverence, serve you.

Reflection questions:

1. In what ways are you blaming yourself and/or others for what happened to your loved one?

2. In what ways are you the recipient of blame from others for what happened to your loved one, and how is it affecting you?

Difficult Conversations

One of the toughest questions to answer in the initial months that came up frequently after my son's death was "how many kids do you have?" What seemed like simple and casual conversation to strangers or acquaintances was a gut-wrenching topic that rubbed salt in the wound. During those conversations I felt like "I was confined and could not escape; my eyes were dim with grief" (Psalm 88). I imagine that couples dealing with infertility or miscarriage go through the same painful experience, which is why I never ask about kids anymore unless the other person brings it up first.

For a long time, I avoided the topic or was not sure how to respond. Should I lie and say that I only have one daughter? Or should I tell the truth and share that I have two children but one got sick and died from a rare disease, which tended to give the conversation a solemn and awkward tone?

My conclusion was that I didn't have to tell everyone at every conversation about my ordeal. Jonah was not going to be offended if I said that I only had one daughter, especially with strangers that I would never talk to again or acquaintances that I didn't know very well.

If I felt comfortable with someone or felt that it was going to be a long-term friendship, then I would share about my experiences and it tended to enrich or deepen the friendship. I could pick and choose when and with whom I would share with.

Psalm 88:1-9

Lord, you are the God who saves me; day and night I cry out to you.

May my prayer come before you; turn your ear to my cry.

I am overwhelmed with troubles

and my life draws near to death.

I am counted among those who go down to the pit;

I am like one without strength.

I am set apart with the dead,

like the slain who lie in the grave,

whom you remember no more,

who are cut off from your care.

You have put me in the lowest pit,

in the darkest depths.

Your wrath lies heavily on me;

you have overwhelmed me with all your waves.

You have taken from me my closest friends

and have made me repulsive to them.

I am confined and cannot escape;

my eyes are dim with grief.

Reflection questions:

1. Under which circumstances do you feel comfortable talking with others about your grief?

2. How will you handle situations when the topic of your loved one comes up when you are caught off guard?

Secondary Losses

Aside from the primary loss of the person you love, the aftermath that follows the catastrophe can result in other losses as well. One of these can be financial loss. Even though money has no comparison with the beautiful life that was lost, it certainly can cause added strain onto an already devastating and stressful experience.

I remember when the debt collectors started calling on behalf of the children's hospital asking for payments, and how unprepared we were to handle that situation. The wounds were still raw and fresh, but already there were more issues to deal with. If this has ever happened to you, you may feel like you are drowning. "All day long they surround me like a flood; they have completely engulfed me" (Psalm 88).

Another type of secondary loss is other relationships in life. Sometimes husbands and wives start arguing or grieve in different ways, and they end up separating. One of the relationships I lost temporarily in my life was my relationship with my mother. She grieved in a very different way, went through a period of denial and withdrawal, and blamed us for a lot of things that happened during my son's hospitalization. We were estranged for over a year after my son died, but thankfully we were able to forgive each other and reconcile.

There are many pieces of the dream of your life that can be shattered when a loved one dies. You may be grieving for not just one person, but multiple relationships or situations at the same time.

Psalm 88:10-18

I call to you, Lord, every day;

I spread out my hands to you.

Do you show your wonders to the dead?

Do their spirits rise up and praise you?

Is your love declared in the grave,

your faithfulness in Destruction?

Are your wonders known in the place of darkness,

or your righteous deeds in the land of oblivion?

But I cry to you for help, Lord;

in the morning my prayer comes before you.

Why, Lord, do you reject me

and hide your face from me?

your terrors have destroyed me.

From my youth I have suffered and been close to death;

I have borne your terrors and am in despair.

Your wrath has swept over me;

All day long they surround me like a flood;

they have completely engulfed me.

You have taken from me friend and neighbor—

darkness is my closest friend.

Reflection questions:

1. What secondary losses have you experienced so far after your loved one passed away?

2. How have these secondary losses impacted your grieving process?

Creative Venting

For me, writing and journaling have always been a way to lessen the emotions of anger, disappointment, and grief. After my son died, I also found other forms of expression that helped me feel better. It started with one of those wine and paint classes I attended with a friend who wanted to get me out of the house. That day, we were painting dream catchers, the ones that are found in the Native American Indian culture.

Something about the act of painting soothed me and made me feel like my son was there with me as I discovered something new. In the months that followed, I created other artwork as well. I continued painting at home on my own. Whales were one of my favorite subjects because of Jonah.

For you, it may be reading, poetry, drawing, playing music or singing songs to release your mourning and grief. God could use some form of creative expression to "lead you to a higher rock" or give you "a refuge, a strong tower" (Psalm 61).

There are a million forms of creativity that have been used throughout history and time to express love, and also loss. The depth of heartbreak that may not be possible to express to others through words could be expressed in other creative forms. With time you will find the right outlet for you.

"When the tears come streaming down your face;
when you lose something you can't replace."

Coldplay – Fix You

Psalm 61:1-5

Hear my cry, O God;

listen to my prayer.

From the ends of the earth I call to you,

I call as my heart grows faint;

lead me to the rock that is higher than I.

For you have been my refuge,

a strong tower against the foe.

I long to dwell in your tent forever

and take refuge in the shelter of your wings.

For you, God, have heard my vows;

you have given me the heritage of those

who fear your name.

Reflection questions:

1. What sources of creativity can you tap into to help with grief, even if you don't consider yourself a creative person?

2. Which musicians or artists can you relate to when it comes to heartbreak and loss?

Different Forms of Grief

Initially I thought I was very much alone and it was unfair of God to deal me such a hard blow at such a young age. With time I found out more about the difficulties that other people were going through. Some of them were mothers who had experienced multiple miscarriages, ectopic pregnancies, or infertility. Some of my friends are going through terrible divorces. I learned that no two experiences of grief are the same, and that is why I hesitate to say "I know how you feel" even if I have experienced grief as well.

My friends who are going through divorce describe it like mourning the dream of a life together with their spouse that has essentially died. They go through the same stages of denial, anger, bargaining, acceptance, and reconstruction. A few of my friends also experienced the death of a parent at a very young age. Their mother or father never saw them graduate from high school and college, or get married.

Grief is such a terrible topic to approach, but it is a universal experience. At one point or another in our lives, we will lose someone we love dearly and it will be a gut punch. Our grief is unique to our individual situation, but also connects us to a broader human experience and forges a common bond. May the Lord be "the strength of his people, a fortress of salvation" (Psalm 28).

Psalm 28:1-2, 6-9

To you, Lord, I call;

you are my Rock,

do not turn a deaf ear to me.

For if you remain silent,

I will be like those who go down to the pit.

Hear my cry for mercy

as I call to you for help,

as I lift my hands toward your Most Holy Place.

Praise be to the Lord,

for he has heard my cry for mercy.

The Lord is my strength and my shield;

my heart trusts in him, and he helps me.

The Lord is the strength of his people,

a fortress of salvation for his anointed one.

Save your people and bless your inheritance;

be their shepherd and carry them forever.

Reflection questions:

1. What types of grief have you seen other people go through?

2. How can you share common aspects of grief with others who can relate to you to find support and understanding?

Social Media

Undoubtedly, if you have social media accounts, they will sharpen the grief that you are already enduring. I used to have a Facebook account and would see pictures of friends' children and birth announcements after my son died. I was happy for my friends, but it was painful enough that I ended up deleting my account so that I could grieve without the additional stress from seeing other people's posts. Eventually I realized that I don't need social media and my life is ultimately better without it. You may want to take the same steps and deactivate your accounts temporarily or delete them permanently.

The truth is that nobody represents his or her life accurately on social media. Everybody posts what they want others to see and depicts life as always being perfect, fun, and interesting. Rarely did I see posts about difficult struggles, losses, or the daily grind. I have noticed that some of my friends are so busy taking pictures and posting online to receive likes and comments that they don't actually live in the moment.

Removing yourself from social media can help you to live more mindfully and be aware of your actual experiences rather than living for others to see. You can always share pictures and thoughts with your friends through text messages or other forms of communication, which can be much more authentic anyway.

With time, you will realize that the true friendships you have in your life don't require social media to thrive. True friends would keep in touch with you no matter the distance or how busy life gets.

Psalm 44:23-26

Awake, Lord! Why do you sleep?

Rouse yourself! Do not reject us forever.

Why do you hide your face

and forget our misery and oppression?

We are brought down to the dust;

our bodies cling to the ground.

Rise up and help us; redeem us because of your unfailing love.

Psalm 69:1-3, 13-18

Save me, O God,

for the waters have come up to my neck.

I sink in the miry depths,

where there is no foothold.

I have come into the deep waters;

the floods engulf me.

I am worn out calling for help;

my throat is parched.

My eyes fail, looking for my God.

But I pray to you, Lord,

in the time of your favor;

in your great love, O God,

answer me with your sure salvation.

Rescue me from the mire,

do not let me sink;

deliver me from those who hate me,

from the deep waters.

Do not let the floodwaters engulf me

or the depths swallow me up

or the pit close its mouth over me.

Answer me, Lord, out of the goodness of your love;

in your great mercy turn to me.

Do not hide your face from your servant;

answer me quickly, for I am in trouble.

Come near and rescue me;

redeem me because of my foes.

Reflection questions:

1. If you have one or more social media accounts, how have they affected you during your season of grief?

2. How can you take a step back from social media to help yourself heal during this time?

Embrace Impermanence

Tibetan monks came to visit our hometown one year at a meditation center. They created their traditional sand mandala artwork, which involves using a tube or funnel to drop grains of colored sand onto a large canvas. The work is extremely tedious and detail-oriented, often taking several weeks or more to complete. Crowds would gather to watch them slowly complete their artwork. The end result was a beautiful pattern made from layers of colored sand placed in intricate designs.

After the sand artwork is completed, the ritual is to destroy the entire thing, wipe the slate clean, and release the sand into a source of water, like a river. This is to illustrate the idea of impermanence.

After my son passed away, I thought of the sand mandalas, their creation and their destruction. I wondered how God could have put so much time and design into creating a beautiful child, but only allow him to live for such a short period of time.

In his book A Grief Observed, C.S. Lewis wrote, "Oh God, God, why did you take such trouble to force this creature out of its shell if it is now doomed to crawl back–to be sucked back–into it?" It seemed cruel and unnecessary, and yet I was reminded that everything is borrowed from God and eventually returns to God. Nothing lasts forever, and life is so fragile. Psalm 39 says that "everyone is but a breath, even those who seem secure."

My loss was a stark reminder of how physical and material things in this world are merely temporary. I have tried to embrace impermanence and appreciate the present moment and the gift of others around me. I have also placed less priority on material possessions because I know that the truly irreplaceable things in life are the people that we love. Often, I meditate on Psalm 39 which says "show me, Lord, my life's end and the number of my days; let me know how fleeting my life is."

Psalm 39:1-7, 12-13

Show me, Lord, my life's end and the number of my days;

let me know how fleeting my life is.

You have made my days a mere handbreadth;

the span of my years is as nothing before you.

Everyone is but a breath,

even those who seem secure.

Surely everyone goes around like a mere phantom;

in vain they rush about, heaping up wealth

without knowing whose it will finally be.

But now, Lord, what do I look for?

My hope is in you.

Hear my prayer, Lord,

listen to my cry for help;

do not be deaf to my weeping.

I dwell with you as a foreigner,

a stranger, as all my ancestors were.

Look away from me, that I may enjoy life again

before I depart and am no more.

Reflection questions:

1. How have you come face to face with the impermanence of life?

2. With time, what are ways that impermanence and fragility have slowly increased your appreciation of the world and people around you?

Ordinary Days

One of the things I missed the most when my son was sick in the hospital was getting to enjoy an ordinary day at home. I realized how much I had taken for granted the quiet, regular days that we got to spend together, doing something simple or even finishing chores. Life had sometimes felt like a "daily grind" or "hamster wheel" with the same routine and tasks every day. Go to work, come home for dinner, go through my son's bedtime routine, clean up, and go to bed.

Now that a catastrophe rocked our entire world and we no longer had that regular routine, I recognized how precious and blessed those ordinary days really were. I missed spending time with each other at home rather than being stuck in the hospital, and getting to hold my son without all the tubes and wires attached to him. I missed playing in his room and seeing his smile and curiosity for life. There were a million ordinary things I missed, especially the freedom of a regular and healthy life that we had outside the hospital.

After my son passed away, I consider this one of the biggest lessons he taught me in life: enjoy ordinary days to the fullest extent and never take a single ordinary moment for granted, because they really are the best kind of days. On ordinary days, "I do not concern myself with great matters or things too wonderful for me, but I have calmed and quieted myself" (Psalm 131).

Cultivate joy and peace in everyday life, especially in the quiet and simple moments when there's not much going on. Adventure and excitement don't have to come from a big event, like traveling for a vacation, buying a new house, or celebrating a special occasion. Every day that you are healthy and alive should be cherished and regarded with the utmost gratitude.

Psalm 131:1-2

My heart is not proud, Lord,

my eyes are not haughty;

I do not concern myself with great matters

or things too wonderful for me.

But I have calmed and quieted myself,

I am like a weaned child with its mother;

like a weaned child I am content.

Reflection questions:

1. What kind of things did you tend to take for granted when your loved one was still alive?

2. With time, what are ways you can honor the memory of your loved one by growing in gratitude for the small things he or she loved in life?

Unity

A friend recently shared her thoughts on what happens to the human spirit after death. She didn't belong to a particular faith or religion, but felt that all souls dissipate and small pieces of that person become parts of other people after death. She thought that maybe I would find her beliefs ridiculous, but it really made sense to me in a way. After my son passed, I felt that he both returned to God the creator and also became parts of people and things I loved here on earth.

Jonah is no longer in one single being. He is part of my daughter. He is in the eyes of beloved family members and friends. He is in every stranger I meet. He is in every patient I treat. He is in the rainbows I see and in every drop of rain. He is in every happy moment and every sad moment. He is within me and every place I go. I perpetually feel his influence and presence with me and in all creation.

Like a river, I feel his life and my own life joined with others around us, pointing towards God's glory, just like it says in Psalm 46: "there is a river whose streams make glad the city of God, the holy place where the Most High dwells."

"Do not stand at my grave and weep

I am not there, I do not sleep.

I am a thousand winds that blow.

I am the diamond glints on snow.

I am the sunlight on the ripened grain.

I am the gentle autumn's rain.

When you awaken in the morning hush,

I am the swift uplifting rush of quiet birds in circled flight.

I am the soft stars that shine at night." [Hopi Prayer]

Psalm 46:1-7, 10-11

God is our refuge and strength,

an ever-present help in trouble.

Therefore we will not fear, though the earth give way

and the mountains fall into the heart of the sea,

though its waters roar and foam

and the mountains quake with their surging.

There is a river whose streams make glad the city of God,

the holy place where the Most High dwells.

God is within her, she will not fall;

God will help her at break of day.

Nations are in uproar, kingdoms fall;

he lifts his voice, the earth melts.

The Lord Almighty is with us; the God of Jacob is our fortress.

He says, "Be still, and know that I am God;

I will be exalted among the nations,

I will be exalted in the earth."

The Lord Almighty is with us;

the God of Jacob is our fortress.

Reflection questions:

1. Which people and places remind you the most of the person you love?

2. How do you feel about an ongoing relationship with the person you love even after they pass away?

Always Within

Recently I was reading an interesting article with a friend who had been through a miscarriage. The article was about a phenomenon called fetal microchimerism, which occurs during early pregnancy when mother and baby share each other's cells. Cells containing DNA from the fetus enter the mother's circulation, persist, and become part of various organs within the mother.

The fetal cells can stay in the mother's body for as long as decades after the birth of the baby. Fetal cells have also been shown to transfer to future siblings. Because of this, I truly feel that Jonah is still part of me and our entire family every day, both spiritually and physically.

When I think about Jonah, he will always remain an innocent baby to me. Psalm 37 says that "the blameless spend their days under the Lord's care, and their inheritance will endure forever." Our infinite spiritual and physical bond, from the womb and beyond, can never be broken by anything. I'll never truly lose my connection with him, not even after death.

Over time, the sting of grief starts to lessen bit by bit. Eventually when you think about your loved one or look at pictures of him or her, you will no longer feel like you're falling into a deep, dark hole. There will always be grief, but it will be easier to recall the smiles, the laughter, and the good times. Tears will no longer be pure despair, but a bittersweet mix of joy and gratitude.

Psalm 37:18

The blameless spend their days under the Lord's care,

and their inheritance will endure forever.

Reflection questions:

1. In what ways do you feel like your loved one is still with you – spiritually, physically, or otherwise?

2. What are ways you can carry your loved one's memory with you in day-to-day life?

Moving Forward

Eventually we may feel some guilt as our grief fades. The grief may even have been what we were holding onto as the last remnants of our relationship with our loved one.

Grief is what kept the memories sharp and pain is what kept our love vivid. As the hold of grief loosens its grip, it may feel like you are losing your connection with your loved one. We may be grappling to hold onto special memories that seem to be disappearing from our minds. As we make new memories and discover joy and laughter again, we have to give ourselves permission to enjoy life again and to find happiness even if it isn't with our loved one.

When our daughter was born a little over a year after our son died, we were grateful to be parents again and to share our love with a new baby. It was bittersweet because we wished that she could have met her brother and that they could have played together and grown up together. Our daughter helped us find joy and laughter again. Even though Jonah can't be here with us, I know he would want us to live our lives to the fullest, with as much happiness as possible.

The best way to honor the person you love is to go into the world and love as many people and things as you can. "Those who go out weeping, carrying seed to sow, will return with songs of joy, carrying sheaves with them" (Psalm 126).

Psalm 60:1-5, 9-12

You have rejected us, God, and burst upon us;

you have been angry—now restore us!

You have shaken the land and torn it open;

mend its fractures, for it is quaking.

You have shown your people desperate times;

you have given us wine that makes us stagger.

But for those who fear you, you have raised a banner

to be unfurled against the bow.

Save us and help us with your right hand,

that those you love may be delivered.

Who will bring me to the fortified city? Who will lead me to Edom?

Is it not you, God, you who have now rejected us

and no longer go out with our armies?

Give us aid against the enemy,

for human help is worthless.

With God we will gain the victory,

and he will trample down our enemies.

Psalm 126

Restore our fortunes, Lord, like streams in the Negev.

Those who sow with tears will reap with songs of joy.

Those who go out weeping, carrying seed to sow,

will return with songs of joy, carrying sheaves with them.

Reflection questions:

1. It is too early to think about this, but eventually, what are small ways you feel yourself opening up to the world again?

2. How can you live in a way that honors the person you love?

Gratitude as a Tribute

When I think of Jonah, I remember there is goodness in this world. There is beauty. There is joy. There is bright light in a world full of darkness. There is something worth living for and something worth fighting for.

As sad and as broken as I am after losing him, Jonah reminds me that there is hope and there is heaven after this life. Despite tragedy, "I remain confident of this: I will see the goodness of the Lord in the land of the living" (Psalm 27). I miss him so much and I can't wait to see him again one day.

I am thankful for the way Jonah brought so much light, laughter, and joy into our lives. He gave me such a clear purpose for my life. I wanted to be a better mother, wife, doctor, person, and to make the world a better place for him. He is still with us and I still live every day to honor his memory.

"What is essential does not die, but clarifies. The highest tribute to the dead is not grief, but gratitude." [Thornton Wilder]

Psalm 27:1-5, 7-9, 13-14

The Lord is my light and my salvation—whom shall I fear?

The Lord is the stronghold of my life—of whom shall I be afraid?

One thing I ask from the Lord, this only do I seek:

that I may dwell in the house of the Lord

all the days of my life, to gaze on the beauty of the Lord

and to seek him in his temple.

For in the day of trouble

he will keep me safe in his dwelling;

he will hide me in the shelter of his tabernacle

and set me high upon a rock.

Hear my voice when I call, Lord;

be merciful to me and answer me.

My heart says of you, "Seek his face!"

Your face, Lord, I will seek.

Do not hide your face from me,

do not turn your servant away in anger;

you have been my helper.

Do not reject me or forsake me,

God my savior.

I remain confident of this:

I will see the goodness of the Lord

in the land of the living.

Wait for the Lord;

be strong and take heart

and wait for the Lord.

Reflection questions:

1. What are the good and pure things that your loved one showed you about the world?

2. With time, how can you rediscover the joy and gratitude for those things?

Planning for the Future

The landscape of your future is forever changed after the loss of someone who was so vital to your plans and dreams. Navigating the process of moving forward and whether to open your heart to the same kind of love and experience again can be a difficult decision.

Since our son Jonah was born with a rare genetic issue, one of the biggest considerations that my husband and I had going forward was whether it was wise to have more children together or not. We had to meet with a genetic counselor and get genetic testing done on both of us. It was a hurdle to predict the likelihood that the same issue would affect a future child, and there was never a clear answer to that, even after extensive testing.

We were afraid that we would have another child sick with the same illness and go through the same tragedy again. On the other hand, not being parents again or having a child in our lives seemed unbearable. Eventually we did have our daughter, who is an incredible miracle and blessing. She helped a lot with our grief, and brought so much joy, laughter, and sunshine back into our lives.

For some couples, having another child may not be a possibility and they have to shift and remake their dreams entirely. I have a lot of friends who are looking at adoption or other possibilities like foster care. May God give you guidance and healing as he leads you into a reimagined future, one that may not be what you were expecting, but is still for the glory of God's bigger story. One way or another, "the Lord gives victory to his anointed" (Psalm 20).

Psalm 20:1-6

May the Lord answer you when you are in distress;

may the name of the God of Jacob protect you.

May he send you help from the sanctuary

and grant you support from Zion.

May he remember all your sacrifices

and accept your burnt offerings.

May we shout for joy over your victory

and lift up our banners in the name of our God.

May the Lord grant all your requests.

Now this I know: The Lord gives victory to his anointed.

Reflection questions:

1. What uncertainties are you facing for the future as you are grieving the past and present?

2. What are some ways to focus on healing in the present instead of looking too far ahead into the future?

Beauty from Ashes

The three-year benchmark recently passed since my son's death and I find myself able to talk more about it with others and even acknowledge how difficult my experience truly was. People are surprised to find out that I ever went through an experience like that. I no longer try to push away my grief or try to get over it. I accept that my grief is with me long-term, and in a way, I even appreciate my grief because it reminds me of my son and the beautiful things he taught me about life. I feel that my heart has been enriched through knowing him, and that I have so much more empathy and understanding for others who are going through difficult situations.

Many of my patients have been through terrible health issues and intensive medical treatments. Having a first-hand experience of what it is like to have my child in the hospital gives me a realistic knowledge of what it is like to be in their position. It is so much more difficult being on the other side of things when you or a family member is sick. I have found that being a good listener and treating everyone with patience and gentleness is as much part of the therapy as the medicines and treatments that we give.

I feel that my grief and mourning are indispensable parts of my life story and human experience, and I consider them an essential part of myself forever. I have seen that joy and peace can still be a part of my life, no matter what happens to me. Psalm 18 says "my God turns my darkness into light." Suffering becomes love. Grief becomes gratitude.

"To have lived at all is a measure of immortality; for a baby to be born to become a man, a woman, to beget others like himself, is an act of faith in itself, even an act of defiance. It is as though every human being born into this world burns, for a brief moment, like a star, and because of its pinpoint of light shines in the darkness, there is glory, there is life." [Daphne Du Maurier]

Psalm 18:28

My God turns my darkness into light.

Psalm 71:1-3, 18-21

In you, Lord, I have taken refuge; let me never be put to shame.

In your righteousness, rescue me and deliver me;

turn your ear to me and save me.

Be my rock of refuge, to which I can always go;

give the command to save me,

for you are my rock and my fortress.

Even when I am old and gray, do not forsake me, my God,

till I declare your power to the next generation,

your mighty acts to all who are to come.

Your righteousness, God, reaches to the skies,

you who have done great things.

Who is like you, God?

Though you have made me see troubles,

many and bitter, you will restore my life again;

from the depths of the earth you will again bring me up.

You will increase my honor and comfort me once more.

Reflection questions:

1. In what ways do you feel a kinship with others who have been through the loss of a loved one?

2. In what ways do you see the vulnerabilities of others because of the vulnerability you have suffered?

Afterword

Looking through my old journals from 2018, I am not sure how I even got through those initial days and months, and survived such a trauma. It is difficult to read the entries from those dark and depressing days. I wouldn't have believed it if I had been able to tell myself that joy, peace, and love would eventually return to my life slowly over time. I see myself and others who have survived grief like phoenixes, burned to the ground slowly into dust, but eventually rising up from the ashes again with a new life. The old me truly died, and a new person took her place.

Often I think it was my guardian angel in heaven who helped me get out of bed every day, go back to work, finish my medical training, and keep going instead of giving up on life after he died. We don't know how resilient our own spirit is until we have been through a crisis and catastrophe.

I am thankful to the friends and family who supported me and the ones who still remember to send us cards on Jonah's birthday and the anniversary of the day he died. I am thankful for having my daughter, who helped me reclaim my identity as a mother and brought a lot of joy and laughter back into our lives. She reminds me so much of my son and reminds me that a piece of him is in every person I encounter during the day—family members, friends, and even strangers.

With every patient I see at work, I remember how difficult it was to be sick or the family member of someone who is sick. I'm still trying to live life the best way I can, and it's like living for two people. May God "be our guide to the end" (Psalm 48).

Psalm 48:14

For this God is our God forever and ever;

he will be our guide even to the end.

Reflection questions:

1. How do you feel your grief changing or staying the same over time?

2. Where do you need additional support during your grieving process?

Recommended Reading

A Grief Observed by C.S. Lewis

Walking with God through Pain and Suffering by Timothy Keller

Healing After Loss: Daily Meditations for Working Through Grief by Martha Whitmore Hickman

Shattered: Surviving the Loss of a Child by Gary Roe

Beyond Tears: Living After Losing a Child by Ellen Mitchell and Rita Volpe, et al.

Always Within: Grieving the Loss of Your Infant by Melissa L Eshleman

Angel Catcher: a Journal of Loss and Remembrance by Kathy Eldon and Amy Eldon Turteltaub

Hearing Jesus Speak Into your Sorrow by Nancy Guthrie

I Wasn't Ready to Say Goodbye: Surviving, Coping, and Healing After the Sudden Death of a Loved One by Brook Noel and Pamela Bair

Healing a Parent's Grieving Heart: 100 Practical Ideas After Your Child Dies by Alan Wolfelt

Every Moment Holy, Volume 2: Death, Grief, & Hope by Douglas Kaine McKelvey

Radiant Rest: Yoga Nidra for Deep Relaxation and Awakened Clarity by Tracee Stanley

ALSO WRITTEN BY THE AUTHOR

The Rheumatoid Arthritis Roadmap

The Psoriatic Arthritis Roadmap

Rheumatology Drug Review: for Boards and Clinical Practice

About the Author

Donica Liu Baker is a rheumatologist practicing the art of medicine in her beloved hometown of St. Louis, Missouri. For her, the best part of being in medicine is having a window of perspective to understand humanity from all walks of life, and getting to see points of view that are different from her own.

She enjoys spending time with her family and friends, writing, and hiking with her dogs Sasha and Coco. She also dabbles in yoga, meditation, practicing piano, singing at her church, and exploring activities around St. Louis city.

Visit www.donicabaker.com.

All proceeds from this book will be donated to help support children who are diagnosed with hemophagocytic lymphohistiocytosis (HLH), a devastating illness with high mortality rate. More research is needed to understand this condition and explore treatment options.

Made in the USA
Monee, IL
30 June 2025

20243298R00069